I AM MEMORY

(Poems)

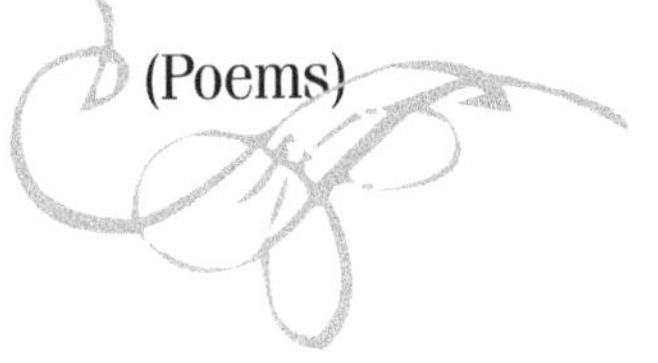

Jumoke Verissimo

LAGOS, NIGERIA

Published in Nigeria in 2008 by DADA Books
an imprint of Design And Dream Arts Enterprises
3/5 Ogun Abewela Street, P.O.Box 130 Ipaja, Lagos, Nigeria.
City Office: 1st Floor, 95 Bode Thomas Street, Surulere, Lagos, Nigeria.
Tel: 234-01-7451990
Mobile: 234-803-3000-499
email: books@dadaenterprises.net,
dreamarts.designagency@gmail.com
www.dadabooks.com

Cover Concept © Emeka Ihejirika
Illustrations: Jummai Ekele
Author's photograph (back cover) © JSK Concepts
Author's photograph (inside back cover) © Chuks Nwanne
Book design © Shina Kelani

ISBN: 978-978-088-065-1

TO
ELEDUMARE
Who willed it,

AND
GBENGA RUFAI
A Dream Deferred.
I'm trying to fill *the* ellipsis.

CONTENTS

ACKNOWLEDGEMENTS

I am lucky to have family and friends who have aided my creativity in ways they wouldn't even know. I thank Papa for his love; Mama, for her strength, my brothers, Seyi, Ajibola and Shola for tolerating my eccentricity. My sisters-in-law and friends, Tolu and Doli-p. Cousin John, Noel, Bennie, Greg Verissimo and Peju and Gbenga Awote for being supportive.

I am grateful to Toyin Adewale-Gabriel, Solomon Huesu, Austyn Njoku, Hycinth Obunseh, who encouraged me to write this collection after I read a piece at the world poetry day event, in 2001. I am immensely grateful for the fortitude when it mattered. Akeem Lasisi and Segun Akinlolu.

My profound gratitude goes to Odia Ofeimun, Prof. Funso Aiyejina for encouraging me at all times. I thank Akin Adesokan and Nduka Otiono for the words of support, voluntary editing and friendship.

I thank, Abimbola Sowemimo, Kyrian Azike, Damilola Famuyide, Nkiru Okafor, Chioma Ezinwa, Igonibo Barrett, Toye Akingbade, Ayo Arigbabu, Tolu Ogunlesi, Chris Ihidero, Yomi Olusegun-Joseph, Albert Obi, Tayo Ogunlewe, Deji Toye, Tunji Azeez (TA), Ropo Ewenla, Ogochukwu Ikenma, Jide Begun (my tolerant editor), Hyacinth Obunseh, Wole Oguntokun, Tola Jimoh, Emeka Ihejirika, Nduka Otiono, Victor Ehikhamenor, Professor

Adebayo Lamikanra, Amiefa Omemu, and Jesse Adeniji for the visions.

I am grateful to the members of Optimom Arts Konsotiom (OAK) for performing Memory lane II (as reparations) at the organised, Ife Poetry Festival.

My sincere appreciation goes to Edun, Awoko, Folake and Damilola for performing my poems at Words & Sound those poetry nights. To all the places that have offered me some space to perform my poems, I am thanks-full.

Olu Okekanye Jahman Anikulapo and Muhtar Bakare for opportunities granted.

'Uncle' Toyin Akinosho and Kayode Ogunbunmi for supporting me when I was 'stagnated'.

The members of Committee for Relevant Art (CORA), Association of Nigerian Authors (ANA), The Guardian Life, who believed in my dreams; Greg Nwakunor, Samson Adeoye, Adeola Adebayo, Chigozie Akanihu, Tosin Oyedepo, Mr. Richards. My friends at Rosabel Advertising… I appreciate you all.

Remi Fashola, Tola Jimoh, Sade Lewis, Paul Hughevu, Tunde Ladega, Nicholas Ibekwe, Munir Ibrahim, Aliyu Bakare, Yusuf Usman-Abubakar for those 'debate' moments.

To the magazines, online and print that have published some of the poems in this collection in different forms, especially, Temenos, The Journal, Canopic Jar, Argotist, Boyne Berries, Bath-tub Gin, Chicken Bones, Mindfire New, Sentinel and the anthologies where some of these poems have appeared in different forms, I say, a very big thank you. To everyone who has supported me thus far, I am immensely grateful. I will not forget.

Memory Lane I

(Of intuition and emotions)

SEQUENCE (Of desire)

Ajani.

Coursing my stream-
ing blood,

cutting my waves of resistance
I become

a stream, the stream,
flowing with no water.

*

I am a stream with no course;
a maiden with charred beads;
memory of kept-away affection.

Ajani.

The beads on my waist,
the heat of my passion,
the pleasure of my ache,

the memory of a
burn
ing groin.

The beads of waiting,
the beads of wanting,
the beads are weighty,

I wait.

My waist pines for your searing,
it is burdened by despised beads
which lightens in your admiration.

In your touch;
my singed waist comes alive,
my beads become my flesh.

Ajani,
you are a kolanut.

My aftertaste of loin-tussle,
sweetness that follows bitterness.

There is no memory without you,
You are the store house of a quest.

*

When tomorrow asks for yesterday,
It is your name I call.

Ajani.
You are the tingling
aftertaste.

You are kolanut.

I taste you.
Do I linger on your tongue too?

Do I tingle?

When amnesia creeps in like surprise rain,
I touch you to remember.

Do you touch yourself to touch me?
Do you remember our touch?

Do you remember the name of fun?
The one we learnt when cast into
the world swallowed by grief.

I know you
Ajani
I learnt you
When we touch, I freeze.

I know your touch
I buried it inside…

You are the secrets of thumbprints:
there are no two Ajani.

If I could find another Ajani,
I would clean these cracked lips
and shut my heart from ache.

But the honesty of your fingers
are memoirs on my skin.

I know your touch, Ajani
it's trapped within my pores
you are the lone memory buried
where fates are moulded into faces.

Your look-alike is emptiness,
your option is a fullness of hurting

I have no choice but you.
I am a memory of hurting
Ajani,
heal me….

I do not know where dreams go,
but I took caution when your footfalls
faded behind me after a drizzle of passion.

You have not stood the test of time,
our memories have. They are fashioned
into annulled-desires,

and now I am learning to gather me,
into a memorable song,
the chorus of echoing desires.

*

Your absence canes me into wanting,
So I've memorised your footfalls.

I know your footfall.
It is passion sketched on my mind,
it is the memoirs of drifting in my head.

I have befriended death

I have sown seeds of discord
at a timed vacation death is away
from me, from you.

*

What protects a man from death?
Memory? Is it memory of riddled riddles?

Or the memory that keeps a man from
remembering how not to swallow his soul?

Ajani.
You shall not die in your prime.
for I remember the name of death.

*

I have memory.

Even when the waters that wetted
our trees of desires dried.

I keep memoirs of flowering,
of budding and harvesting.

Ajani,
you have pinched my desires
I hold my breath
I am memory.

*

Peel your pericarp of doubt
taste the conviction in our touch
and let your loins throb in memory.

Or have you tasted the likeness of our pleasure?

If the past were three-dimensional,
our yesterday was a composite volcano
exploding into a mass of questions

it was not me
it was not your way
it was the sequence of forgetfulness.

Ajani
remember when my ache(s)
troubled your sleep
till you wet yourself on me...
the love-mares in the deep of the night

your name
my face

your touch
my breathe

our eyes
my mind

those times, brightened visions…

Ajani,
my ambition is
to have your eyes in mine
to hold your hands and hope
to keep your lips on mine
to wear your heart in mine
and do nothing.

But, you confuse me
Ajani
you torment me

You are a haughty riddle!

Do I bite your thoughts?

Do you flip through the pages
of our unwritten memoirs?

I am a tendril
Do I rest on you?

It is time to ask that our memory
will not sink into hate,

that evil shall pocket its own grief
that you lead and breed only the best.

You will not die in your prime,
may tongues that wag, not tramp you down.

Ajani,
we are not strangers. We are friends.
This world is a race, we're a trace.

Ajani,
if you will not smile
on the banquet table
of rotund cheeks of 'thieving' politicians

Insincere friends with callous ways
smile for me, and bed peace

Ajani,

Let them talk till they wilt

I am your memory.

Memory Lane II

(Of an enchained tale)

Association

I am the memory
of asking and not getting
of seeing and not beholding,

of brokenness
waiting for succour,
and fantasising recompense.

Times have not changed
pain has; it has grown bolder.

My desires have gathered moth; it's a
thickened skin; it is a spectator

of communal hurting, of sour desires,
of minds slivered while forgetting

of many years of trampling; and
thirst in abundance of water.

*

I know the stories of ancestors
of praying against a dance of ridicule
of fame exchanged for a bath of shame.

I am memory;
of cheap labour and chipped shoulder.
even now, times have not changed…

*

I am the memory
of souls who voyaged
into seas of persecution,
seeking liberation in bloodied ties.

I am memory;
of passages
leading home to discontent,
of passages,
of dry bones that failed to rise
when bitterness scourged their strength.

I am the middle passage;
reflections of the Atlantic,
the mirror of a century's groan.

*

I am memory... of death
I know the names of death.

Disillusion is a name we call death,
anger is a companion that celebrates him.

The Middle Passage is death,
disease, the dame that courts her,
ambition, an ally that lures her,
war, the mother that births her,
I am a clan's dearth.

I have the memory of death
of passages and passers-by, passing
trust, miming regrets, about parted
spores, unreturned and unchecked
largesse and kindness in blindfolds.

I am two, that's one in a clime of guilt,
I am the guilt of the trader and the traded.

*

I am the trader, who sees difference as conquest,
the traded who brands humility as servitude.

*

I am the transit
I know what it is
I know what it is not
I know what it is not to be.

I am the Middle Passage;
lengthened grievances of legless accusations,
of someone's father minding unfatherly businesses.

The middle passage,
a long search for
distancing, distance and distances.

Let those who hide remember those who find,
for I am memory...of gin bringers; sin-bringers.

I am a mirror;
reflections of guilt and groans.

I am a cloth,
civilised cover for societal splotch
an age-sown pain,
that stays, that stains.

I am the scattered leaves of an oak tree,
fertilising the grounds of strange whims.

I am the colour of a skin,
the essence of a being,
bargaining nature for sameness
whenever skin measures human intelligence.

I am memory.

Retrospection

I know brokers of diamond dreams, they
copulate in mines when mates are in fetters.

I know IMF;
International Misery Fellows, whose
kindness borders on wretchedness.

I know desire that flowered trauma,
tales of protection weaving destruction,
stories of UN-desirable aid-givers,
World Bank of unmeasured miseries.

I am the waters where anger has shushed voices,
into a stem of bitterness, into a tree:
two stems; with three branches,
the knower, the-knowing and the know-not.

I am Diaspora, the fresh ire, of
erring sires who flipped destiny.

I am ancestors who
embraced hope, but found
discord rooted in posterity.
I am the memory
of Sierra Leone

serial loan of enchanted bitterness
of Liberia
lying burials of ailing serenity
of Sudan
sedating hunger and impaired righteousness.

I am those places
where death is an appraisal of hope,
I know the home of familial disconnect
where ties of belonging are soups of blood,
where happiness farms anticipation; harvests sorrow.

I know fathers who are
heedless fighters of kindred enmity.
I know everything that means nothing.

*

I know *they* voyaging into waters of amnesia,
slipping into an eternity of jumbled history,
stalling yesterday's possibilities in shipwrecks,
overboard burying, plantation rapes, skin abuse.

I am the memory of ships;
Mercy, Jesus, Ann, Desire...
where wo(man) evolved into
rotting meat sighing for death.

I know Royal African Company;
makers of Royalty Alienated companion
ship, traders of serfdom.

I am the next-of-skin to plantation workers,
next-of-kin to worldly neglect,
I am memory.

I tell stories of a question-marked century,
of history's untreated patients, whose
memoirs of festering sores ache to heal.

I wear regalia of prayers,
murmur hunger-sagged dreams:

*

I know the story of a century's scar,
the history of a noiseless brawl,
forgetfulness worming a race into discord.

ships that rode ignorance to shores of abuse

I know when conscience in a dance of shame
asked, 'who should be blamed for its woeful name?'
Who does it blame for his mother's nakedness?
A child who sells off her clothes,
or strangers who peddle her pride in glee?

*

I, recall of aching joints,
of passions, of pain, of un-priced productions.

I know of
wounds that don't heal, of scars and foes,
desert sun and lash from arrogant men
whose anger against self, repels mercy.

I am the welt of the world,
the caustic memories of labourers,
whose inheritance is slummed fathers.

I am the memory of a time.

*

I am the 15th century:
the beginning that tarries,

sealed screams of serfs,
aching freedom in shark-waters,
history written on the conscience of ignorance
I am Mercado De Escravos
Calabar
I am Elmina Castle[1]
I am the shores

of unfinished orgasms.

I, Trinidad and Tobago
trinity; whose unit is apart from its unity
I, Cuba,
cubic dimension of racial drunkenness,
the lost
the found
the forgotten.

I, shoring an enslaved race to visibility.
I, the riddle of continuity.

*

I am memory,
riding on unbroken waters of misery,
            under the weight of memorial greed,

on shores where anger is a souvenir
where seas tell tales of brokenness,

and stories with ends that stretch,
live with meanings that diverge.

I the memory of a memory;
of manila, cowries, gunpowder, guns…
pittances battered for possibilities.

I am the guns; those
enslavers of a race's probabilities
I, fragments of togetherness
the suicide of desire.

I am hurt that slights words.
I, the memento.

Mnemonics

Forgetfulness is the villain's not the victim's.
I do not forget, for;
I am death and life,
infliction in a festival of transgression.
I, the whips, chains, ships, waters, sand, and cowries...
begging the Atlantic to massage centuries of hurt

I am the sigh wishing the years
that merged hate with trust will melt away.

*

I hear the groans of the Atlantic-
the lashes against the shores are in anger.
Overflowing waves are not the sea on duty,
they are the Atlantic sighing, wishing, wailing out in regret.

I tell stories of inglorious partings,
of memories signed into scarred backs.

*

I know islands and land-masses of familial discords,
I now hear the Atlantic echoing...

Telling tales of inglorious partings, when
memories tore into bare backs, while

peace, pissed over itself in fear, and
intimacy shattered into binary compounds;

one in two-fold; the Diaspora thatsamedifference.
I wipe my hands over the cheeks of glamour-ills.

As this memory begs to heal,
chipped shoulders and cheap labour.

Time has not changed
pain has; it has grown bolder

*

I know the chants of helpless waters,
the muted songs of sunken slaves,
I learnt a new song on desolate shores:

In songs of the sea I hear tales of a city,
a generation of waters named with shame.

I am the shores
I know Calabar,

I know you *Agbede Greme;*[2]
Agbcdc's farm: the ancient safe of tales
where generations' shed shells,

You; *agbadagiri,* now Badagry,
the bereaved antiquary
weaving a face with no past
you have lost it in scarless yester-shame.

You are the maiming earth
that lured men into wailing seas,
you are a reminder
the retention of our past.

I ride on the tears of the seas,
on men with merchandised minds
of a race that raced into retardation, while its
generations faded like darkness consumed at dawn.

I am the middle consumed by the beginning;
though time has wiped out my grudge:
times have not changed
pain has: it has grown bolder.

I billow effortlessly into reggae of impoverishment.

I am a generation of grief,
a generation of rift,
a generation on fief,
a generation adrift.

RETRIEVAL

How do we awaken a sea in coma?
How do we remove the soul of a generation's memory
that's dissolved and dried in the heart of a million sores?

True, some pains surpass words…

The memory of a pain that pines for esteem,
a pain cracked in every physical embrace
Will my memory brighten a darkness incited clime?

I stagger for stability though drunk with chaos
I search for:
broken ties of commonality,
unseen cries of individuality,
shattered dreams of mentality,
abused sights of humanness.

I am the voice across the Atlantic
the eyes that sail home despondent

I am memory.

Memory Lane III

(Of places and people)

THE RAPE
(For the Niger-Delta, Nigeria)

This discharge; is it oil or blood?
or conscience pricking vulvas
into piles of mangrove guilt?

This discharge;
consuming hymens of virgin skies;
enraging, flaring splintered hopes.

This discharge,
from a fluid-less pen
is: oil or blood?

Releasing hate into sacred vulvas,
ruffian thrusts divest virgins of honour;
leaving strife-seeds on endowed-wombs.

Is it oil or blood that strained the foetus
from the wombaborting oracular
births, with cordless umbilical?

These days,
aged vulvas live in fear of perverts,

weakened thighs plead change from
violent thrusts on impotent will.

Vulvas with many-name contagions;
breed fear of *un*reached orgasm.

Smelly privates lack confidentiality,
they are a meal-time discourse.

These once-virgin thighs: over-raped
plead for menopause…

*

Why does ambition in the
South-South[3] go South-South?
Is it because they are in the South?

or because their vulva is looking south,
so promises are heading south,
all is going down, getting drowned.

Their dreams go South-South
anger goes South-South
thoughts drift South-South:
against renewal and contemplation.
Is it this oil or blood
that makes desires head South-South?

*

Here.
Deformed skills and tired anger,
molest dominant wills,
time speaks against the call of the oracle.

Why is MOSOP[4] - soppy?
Is it this oil: this blood
    that has leeched its peak?
what is MEND[5] - mending?
Is it this oil: this blood
    that has bleached its own?

Is it the plea to head South-South
and meet patriots of better times only,

Those leeches
those b*oil* companies,
those diseased, whose partner
ship, steers our blood to riot
those who steered Boro[6], Wiwa[7] to no return.

Those woes
who sucked our rivers dry.

See what we have become
children from same vulva,
see what we have become
see marsh, see river,

apart aloof
    the river shies from the marsh
like they share no watery relations.

It's time this oil be their blood;
and turn against them.

The sword disregards the smith in battle,
this blood will oil their joy to ache.

This oil will be their blood,
this blood is oil.

Those Rapists,
this birth will turn against them.

If you rig a condom to prevent procreation,
I shall burst its tip and yet make babies.
Rapist
if you do not copulate for affection,
you reciprocate past affliction.

This oil is blood,
this oil
this blood
will flow as it should flow.

This vulva must drip fresh blood,
our menopausal dream shall ovulate,
it shall menstruate;
not-clotted blood, blackened shame
sign of early aging and destitution.

This meddle of affairs on arrears
this oil
this blood
this what?
this confusion of signs and times....

This discharge of rot
that persists.

This seething anger has spilled over
on our farms of hope,
in our streams of strength.

The untimely thrust in underage vulvas,
deflowered our ancestral affinity,
killing posterity and famished wills.

Now,
the raped vulva pleads for menopause,
oversexed vulvas beg for a sex-change,
against violence, your thrust on their impotent will.

STILL BREATHING
(For Dafur, Sudan)

I exist against the selection of hunger,
the gauntness more vocal than the media.

I live in a world that cursed the era of Hitler,
but now bows into memories of his passion.

I stand, bent, resisting a fall into extinction,
even when the days I live, swing into

            dark years. I live, gasping rotten air,
holding bland lives thrown at me in random.

I float in the depth of shallow emotion
keeping sanity soldered with brokenness,

Insanity and death are choices,
left in my basket of humaneness,

and as minds fight to breathe amidst,
constellated anger of a craving people.

I keep up against the dearth of everything,
for pain is scarce and vacuum is a resort.

THE DISPOSED

(For Ken Saro Wiwa and the eight[8])

One November the sun leapt into
a man's heart and scorched
mercy into a caked bristle; reason died.

He forced Ken into a roped slumber,
he envenomed his flesh into ash;
befriended Ken's kin and soiled their robe…

*

Before slumber, Wiwa voiced that his
Forest of Flowers would not like the
Quagga become another fabled beauty.

Though hung and burnt, Ken's mind trudged,
warring the wilting senses of furrowed minds
he burnt incense of greed-astray in scorched souls.

*

And for *shell*ers[9] of dreams, partakers of grief,

Who understood Ken
Who knew his yearn
Who saw it penned...

The sickness of their heads bullied some thoughts

into quiet; it sizzled brains and splintered wisdom,
so every understanding lost its understanding.

*

Now I, memory of a clan, memoirs of a time,
muttered prayers, claiming death for the torturer.
I appealed that death be pummelled to silence,
          because it filched Ken: *the* unread book…

*

Had I struck a deal with God
before that November.

Had I struck a deal with God,
against that November.

I would avoid the crucifixion on *that* November,
I would call *father, father have you forsaken me…*

I would murder the goat, who *abashed*[10] conscience,
I would batter the existence of his descent...

I have not struck a deal with God
the descendants of Satan abound as rulers,
times are veiled, nothing has changed
men still wear robes of ill-thirst and injustice.

*

Ken,
dreams are treading *On a Darkling Plain*[11]
that's where alien greed has landed ambition.
Brain with content now burn with discontent
Men roast as forgotten meals in kerosene blasts
toddlers abduct foreigners into sacred mangroves…

I know
black market stark dearth charred deaths
I know
cooked flesh booked fates timed lives
I know
Many endings where the mind
wears a robe of anger against injustices

*

The woodcock for its children's sake
cast its feathers in a flood of dye

The woodcock for its children's sake
cast its wings in the fluid of camwood

Ken for the sake of Ogoni, you birthed
dreams in the ashes of defilers:
I may be dead but my ideas will not die [12]
So you said in 1995.

You fought that the greed of strangers'
will not turn our own as hounds

I clutch your words as guard:
They are not going to arrest us all[13]... so you said.

They haven't arrested us all
They can't arrest us all…

They've arrested conscience,
convalescence lives in our hearts.

FOR THE DISPOSSESSED

(*M.K.O Abiola;* In memory of June 12)[14]

Moshood[15]
this is memory

chanting and healing clots
of yesteryear's wound, from

shaming nobles wobbling
in Nigeria's conscience cart

*

I remember you
not as the hero disrobed
in a fit of madness
but the madness death-robed
into a myth of valour
You've left a triple score
with gun trotting bumpkins
round cheeks
            round necks
                        round heads
                                    and round brains

Those smuggled historians with
square cheeks
            square necks

square heads
and square brains

The lunatics plummeting,
drifting into bigger daftness

They have left no
grief but brief pain

Abiola
you filled our numbness, and
rebelled against the yoke of tyranny
Now, the cheat must pay the cheated

*

In this ocean of evil
I struggle to the shores of atonement

with pledge, your side I take:
the fool must pay the fooled

*

Forget their forgetfulness
Olawale[16]
your heart is preserved
Their forgetfulness...
gathered demise for whimsies
victory for our incantations

They did not know forgetfulness
was the bane of the duck
it remembered not to part its toes

They did not know
forgetfulness was

the bane of the sheep
it left its incisor in its mother's womb....

*

Convention infuriates an insane
he'd wear clothes at night
walk naked at daybreak

Moshood,
you left venom in their midst
now lives are imbued in spite

*

They have become,
fishermen wishing to be firemen
farmers hoeing soils with the phantasm of the gunner
hunters preying to become hunted

In the demise of pride
these men eat yam tubers
sprouting from the lips of boys,
with loyalty shifted into bags of lies.

Even sons parade fathers
whose madness tow shame
to rumple the truck of peace...

Till the edges are smoothed
I will not forget.

THE LOSS

(for Cousin Gbenga cut down by armed robbers).

I dress my skin in grief, wear a cap of loss
chew bones and bones of memories, and
earth carcass of unearthed desires.

I told untold and retired stories,
love messages never passed; in tears
my eyes cursed restrainers of endowments,

of *my* gift thrown into the hands of a million
madnesses. My bereaved face bleeds with
wailing, hoping it immortalises the lost.

I scavenge the details of an abrupt end
carve gutters on my brows
I hush pain in the noise of sorrow,

as mementoes eat leftover emotion,
so even breathing becomes
configured into waves of living torture.

I remember last meetings, familial connections,
those years we spent together form a
clod of mist in the corners of my eyes.

I wait for solace
I still remember.

THE SILENCED

(For Bola Ige, Funso Williams and
the unsolved deaths.)[17]

I know them;
the counterfeit disillusion,
the cannibals who feed on country-dream,
they who will swallow their hearts as last supper.

I know them;
silent grief-bearers,
The noise of their quiet,
I pray, deafens their ears.

I remember;
The laws of the murdered;
grief remains a stone throw from killers.

THE ABUSED
(The Nigerian Youth)

See the baby I have remained,
two decades and more I suck
sagging breasts, brag over puerility
I sing songs of deliriums and letdowns:

parents listen to your children
We are the leaders of tomorrow…[18]

I have listened to old ills
fed on chipped heels
rode on hunch backs
slept in crooked arms…

My fluttering eyes remain nascent
fights are grounded in snailing times,
time for oldness crawl at poverty pace,
I'm the same until blinded with age
I am neither here nor there
(I have been left to wear nappies)
I can neither hear nor dare.

I'm a woman yet a girl; a man yet a boy,
hiding behind the lies of convening fathers;
failers who welded my dreams with brokenness
deleting and rewriting tortures in my head.

I weave ambitions into fatigue,
I bother into no-next-level. For
each day I learn that there is no
place to nestle my woes.
I will not forget.

The conundrum of a People

What land is waiting for the skies to rain bread?

Memory Lane IV

(Of falseness and being)

False Memory
The Riddle:

This my aging delight…
of birth
of worth
of earth
of strung
lamentation….

Of birth
I share ache and unnumbered hours,
Of worth
I bear fake seconds of ecstasy,
Of earth
I dare a stake to endless calamities.

I am war…

*

War that makes the world go bland.
I house utopia and dystopia, and
in thin slits I create jealousy,
house subjugation, and
rearing servitude into advantages?

I am *the* thing.
The memory that clothes
erections into digressions; I break
rigidity into involuntary flaccidity.

*

I am the receiver,
the container, the abuse-donor

I, language of forced patience
the torture; the unsolved equation

the joy of grated freedom, the
anger in a platter of condescension

I have earned contraceptive freedom
I stand apart from wholeness.

*

Maker (are you there?)

There is haggling over
my existence

a pen
is rewriting my ambitions

a vain pro/test
against my resolutions

Maker (are you there?)
Is there a mistake?

Does variance mean disparity?

*

I am memory.

INDEX

1. Names of Atlantic slave trading posts.
2. Native name of Badagry, a coastal border town in Lagos State.
3. Description of a region of the south of Nigeria.
4. Movement for the Survival of Ogoni People (MOSOP)
5. MEND: Movement for the Emancipation of the Niger-Delta
6. BORO: Nigerian, Niger-Delta activist.
7. WIWA: Ken Saro-Wiwa, Nigerian, Niger-Delta activist and leader of MOSOP, hanged on General Sani Abacha's orders in 1995 with eight other activists.
8. WIWA and Eight: coinage for the Niger-Delta activists hung on the orders of despotic Nigerian Head-of-State, General Sani Abacha.
9. Shell*ers*: Coined from Shell one of the companies often accused for the despoliation of the Niger-Delta in Nigeria.
10. Coined from the name of erstwhile Nigerian dictator Gen. Sani Abacha, on whose orders Ken Saro Wiwa was killed.
11. *On a Darkling Plain* is the title of one of Ken's books on the Nigerian Civil War, fought between 1967-1970.
12. Quote from Ken Saro Wiwa during his lifetime
13. Quote from Ken Saro Wiwa during his lifetime
14. MKO Abiola-- He was the acclaimed winner of the June 12, 1993 presidential elections in Nigeria. The election was adjudged the freest and fairest in Nigeria, before it was annulled. Abiola died in detention.
15. First name of MKO Abiola. From the initial M.
16. Last name of MKO Abiola
17. Bola Ige was former Attorney General of Nigeria, Funso Williams was a governorship aspirant. They were assassinated at different times, in what remains, two of the most alarming assassinations in Nigeria. Their killers are yet to be apprehended.
18. From a popular chorus in Nigeria

www.ingramcontent.com/pod-product-compliance
Ingram Content Group UK Ltd.
Pitfield, Milton Keynes, MK11 3LW, UK
UKHW021933190726
13853UKWH00004B/1423

9 789780 880651